Knitting

THIS IS A CARLTON BOOK

Published in 2015 by Carlton Books Limited
20 Mortimer Street
London W1T 3JT

10 9 8 7 6 5 4 3 2 1

Text and Design © Carlton Books Ltd 2015

A CIP catalogue record for this book is available from the British Library.

ISBN 978 1 78097 420 0

Text by Tessa Evelegh
Senior Executive Editor: Lisa Dyer
Managing Art Director: Lucy Coley
Picture Researcher: Emma Copestake
Production Controller: Janette Burgin
Designer: Emma Wicks
Cover design by Lisa Layton

Printed in Dubai

You **Tutorial**

Knitting

$\mathbb{Q}$

► Your guide to the best instructional YouTube videos

CARLTON BOOKS

Contents

Introduction   6

Tools of the Trade   8

The Basics of Knitting   14

Knitting Styles and Stitches   28

Correcting Errors   42

Shaping   48

Cabling   59

Lace Knitting   68

Colour Work – Stripes and Intarsia   79

Fair Isle Colour Knitting   87

Finishing and Care   96

Decorative Details and Projects   108

Credits   128

INTRODUCTION

How to use this book

Can't knit, but long to knit? If the idea of learning to manipulate needles and yarn has always seemed somewhat daunting, this book could change all that. You might have been put off in the past for many reasons. Diagrams in books can be confusing. Or perhaps the person who taught you might not have been on hand to answer questions when you needed them most. But none of that matters here. Each video in this book has been chosen for its close-up view of exactly where the needles and yarn need to be placed for each different stitch or technique. And you can go back time and again to check a new how-to, even if it's the middle of the night. Or check out what to do if you have a problem mastering a stitch or the knitting just doesn't look quite right.

At its simplest, knitting really is dead easy and once you know how to cast on, cast off, knit and purl, you can begin a wonderful journey of fabulous colours and textures. With a little practise, you'll find you can knit almost anywhere: while watching TV, in the doctor's waiting room, on a bus or train.

Start with something simple, such as a scarf or cowl, using big needles and yarn for a quick result. We've even included several videos with fun, free start-to-finish tutorials for easy-knit pieces. Once you have more experience, you'll be able to create beautiful fabrics that can be made into garments, accessories and even soft furnishings.

Become a knitter and you'll be joining a wonderful tradition dating back centuries. There are videos showing exactly how to master ancient knitting skills such as Aran and Fair Isle, which you can then re-interpret in your own way to make gorgeous garments that are right for you right now.

The repetitive, rhythmic movements of knitting have been shown to aid concentration, reduce anxiety, boost memory and improve dexterity.

But beware – once you start, you could well become addicted to knitting!

How to View the Clips

Each entry is accompanied by a QR code, which you can scan with your digital device using apps such as Quick Scan, QR Reader or ScanLife. Alternatively there is a short URL address which you can type into your browser. Unfortunately the adverts preceding some of the clips are unavoidable but it's usually possible to skip them after a few seconds.

TOOLS

of the Trade

Understanding Yarn

 Donna gets down to the nitty gritty of knitting yarns

From fibre content and weight to how to substitute yarns in patterns, Natazia's Donna covers just about everything you need to know about knitting yarns. Showing us examples of each type, she explains what to choose for different kinds of projects, and directs us to label information that will also help with decision-making when buying. She even explains how to work out the yarn weight if it is not marked on the label. Although her channel is more about crochet than knitting, this is nevertheless one of the most comprehensive videos on knitting yarns.

http://youtu.be/JvLykvVV2sk

How to Read a Yarn Label

A guided tour around
the label wrap

Yarn labels are packed with loads of valuable information, from the fibre content and laundering instructions to what size needles you should use. Using the simplest, most obvious visual – a yarn label itself – Robotminion highlights each section or symbol as she explains what it means and how you can read the information in relation to your project. No need to check out the rest of her channel, this is the only video that has anything at all to do with knitting. Maybe that's why it works: no fancy diagrams or charts, just the information we really need.

http://youtu.be/ASs2ZzM5WQI

How to Make Yarn from T-Shirts

Turning old T-shirts
into cool yarn

T-shirt fabric cuts up into such cool yarn that some
high-end manufacturers buy in factory end-of-line
T-shirts and fabric offcuts specially to turn into yarn.
You don't have to go that far – your own wardrobe
might be a great source or, as Trisha from Upcycled
Stuff suggests, you can trawl thrift shops for T-shirts
in fabulous shades to make up your very own
fashion yarn collection. Follow this tutorial for tips
on how to source the best T-shirts and how to cut
long continuous lengths of yarn, plus the easy trick
that neatens the edges.

Choosing Knitting Needles

Everything you ever need to
know about knitting needles

For nearly ten minutes, Elsteffo has us mesmerized by knitting needles. She doesn't just show, she tells! Which to use when? Well, not long ones if you're in a confined space, she suggests, as anyone sitting close to you might not appreciate the jabbing. They might find clicky metal ones annoying too! From a knitter's point of view, we discover when to use sharp pointy ones, when to use blunter ones, when slippy and when not so slippy. We see all the materials – metal, bamboo, plastic – and all the types: straight, double pointed and circular. Her one omission is cable needles – though you can (and many people do) substitute small double pointed needles (see also Cabling, pages 59–67).

http://youtu.be/yuqXEe1dr6g

The Essential Toolkit

Very Pink Knits opens up her box of knitting tools

Take a real life whistle-stop trip with Very Pink Knits through her remarkably tiny plastic (pink, of course) box of tricks packed with an astonishing amount of intriguing things. She starts by pulling out an even smaller (pink) plastic box sub-divided for tapestry needles and stitch markers, followed by a ruler/needle gauge, measuring tape, row counter, stitch holders of various types, scissors, pen, cable needles and a funny little fixer tool. The final "rabbit that gets pulled out of the hat" is the beauty kit: hand cream, nail file and lip stuff (just because). Phew! Take a look. It's worth it.

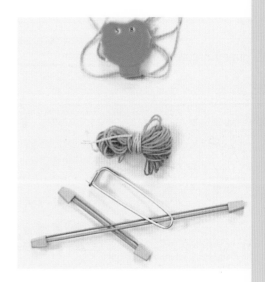

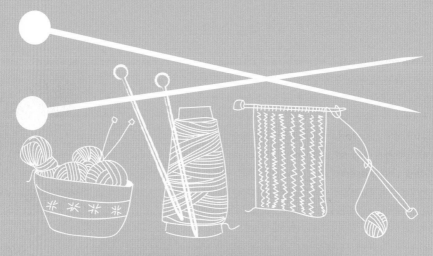

THE BASICS

of Knitting

Cast On, Thumb Method

 Casting on the
easy peasy way

This is such a simple cast-on method, it's the one Wool and the Gang teach to little children. All you need is one knitting needle, your thumb and the yarn and away you go. Worked with a ball of super chunky yarn, it's easy to see exactly what is going on in this stylish video, shot against a simple white background. The presentation is succinct and to the point, explaining the pros and cons of the method as well as how to do it. All swiftly executed in less than a minute and a half!

The Long Tail Cast On

The knit-whizz way
to get started

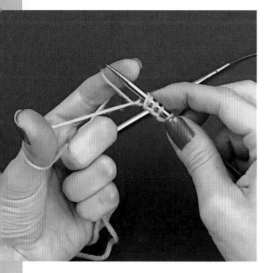

To the uninitiated, this neat, whizzy way to cast on looks like cats' cradles on speed with the added complication of a knitting needle. Good thing, then, that Knitpicks goes through how to work it step by step, and then shows us again and again, because, to be frank, even demonstrated slowly, you miss it the first time. But those who are practised at long tail cast on can whip through it almost without looking. So if you've always wondered how, but never dared to ask, you no longer have to. It's all here!

http://youtu.be/kn4rcAnnS7U

Casting On, Needle Method

Steady-as-you-go,
classic cast on

This is a useful standard method of casting on, providing a stable base for your knitting. Starting with how to do the slip-knot, it's a great one for beginners because you don't have to calculate how long to leave the tail, yet it's more stable than the basic thumb method. Another advantage is that it doesn't require much more skill than a simple knit stitch. It is explained and demonstrated here clearly and succinctly using large needles and double-knit yarn that's easy to see.

Very Stretchy Cast On for Rib

Stretching to the limit
from the very start

Many people just use their favourite cast-on method for rib. But this way makes a wonderful, very stretchy edge for smarter rib with a more comfortable and elastic fit. As the cuffs and welts of most sweaters are in rib, once you know how to knit this stretchy ribbing, you could find yourself using it loads. Watch carefully – the muddle of yarn action can be difficult to understand, but it is considerably easier to follow than the long-tail cast on. If you don't quite get it for any reason, take a look at Tillybuddy's longer version video on stretchy cast on, which she made for extra clarity.

http://youtu.be/iTIBTm0QL6A

Working a Knit Stitch (English Style)

The foundation stitch
for all knitting

The knit stitch is the very foundation of knitting. This short video shows how to knit English style, or, as some people call it, the "throwing" method. This is a good video to watch because it not only shows you the technique close up, but also shows a long shot so you can see the rhythm and speed of an experienced knitter. This is important because the different styles affect the speed of knitting. Many beginners are taught this basic throwing style as it's easy both to understand and to accomplish, but some people think it is slow to begin with. As this video shows, speed comes with experience. Some throwers find that by holding the needles differently, they can get even quicker (see page 30).

Making a Purl Stitch (English Style)

Knit's mirror-image
teammate

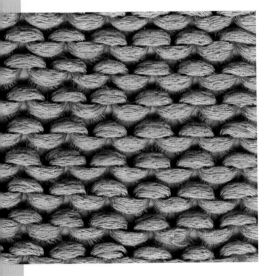

Purl is knit's best friend. These two stitches work together in different combinations to make up all the other fancy (and not-so-fancy) knitting stitch patterns. This video shows clearly how to work a purl stitch using the basic Throwing style where the left hand comes off the needle. These two tutorials work well together as the first shows that if you knit all the rows, you'll get garter stitch. (You also get garter stitch if you purl every row.) If you alternate knit and purl rows, you'll end up with stocking (stockinette) stitch, which you can see when she turns over the knitting at the end of the video.

Stocking (Stockinette) Stitch (st st)

Knitting's favourite
basic stitch pattern

We all think of standard jersey (whether it's hand knit, factory knit, or even T-shirt material) as that stretchy fabric made up of loads of little Vs. Which it is! But if you are working back and forth on two needles you can only get that effect by working alternate rows of knit stitches and purl stitches, which is demonstrated here by Howcast. She also explains that if you are working in the round, you don't have to bother with purling as you're always working on the front of the fabric. So just knit around and around and around to get the classic jersey effect.

Basic Rib (K1 P1 Rib)

Easy stretch for wrists,
waists and necklines

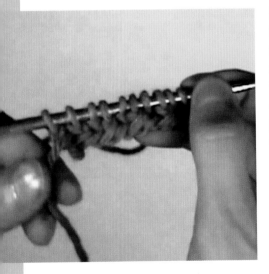

Basic rib comes high up there in the list of classic knitting skills. Just like stocking stitch, you use alternate knit and purl but this time, instead of alternating every row, you alternate every stitch. This video shows how to do that and how to work out which stitch you need to do next, even if you're just picking up your knitting after a break. You'll want to learn this: most knitting has ribbing in it somewhere for stretchiness. Also it makes up into a pleasing flat fabric, so rib is great for scarves, which make brilliant beginner projects.

http://youtu.be/pTA29m8jlzQ

How to Cast Off (Bind Off)

The finishing line

Here's how to finish off each piece once you've finished knitting it. In an attractive, well-produced video, the technique is presented especially for beginners, and so includes really useful extra information that seasoned knitters might take for granted. For example, beginners are very likely to cast off their work too tightly because that's just how it naturally works unless you consciously decide to loosen the tension. We are reminded of this in the tutorial so there's no excuse for inadvertently reducing the stretchiness of the finished edge.

How to Cast Off (Bind Off) in Ribbing

Giving the finish
some stretch

The stretchiness of ribbing, around a neckline, for example, needs to be carried through in the casting off and this video shows and tells us exactly how to do that. It also explains why the result will be so much neater and more pleasing to the eye. Shot finishing off an almost completed sweater, rather than on a little swatch, this evocatively shot video conveys that wonderful moment when you've almost finished a fabulous textural piece of knitting that realizes your original vision.

http://youtu.be/ObMG_EVAnas

The Three Needle Cast Off (Bind Off)

The no-sew way to join and finish
two pieces at the same time

Here is a great way of seaming two pieces together and casting them off at the same time. It's neat, it's easy and it's great for knitters who hate sewing (which many *do*!) A clear, easy-to-follow video that's all finished in just over three minutes, Purl Soho goes into plenty of detail, starting with which way your needles need to be pointing. She works in a contrast yarn so we can see clearly what is going on and just how neat the finished result can be.

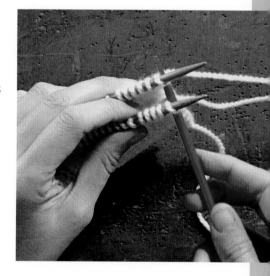

Tension Squares and Knitting Gauge

Doing the maths to get it right

Knitting tension (or gauge) squares might feel like the most boring activity on earth when all you want to do is get going, but it is *definitely* the key to project success. If your square doesn't come out the specified size and you just go ahead and knit the project, you'll get into all kinds of problems. If the gauge is wrong, the garment could end up too wide or too skinny-tight and all the shaping will come out wrong. So take the time to knit a tension square and make the adjustments needed. This is a bit of a complicated maths problem with three variables: the needle size, the yarn size and your own knitting tension. In this video, Debbie Stoller explains all.

http://youtu.be/xJx5krxtPsl

Choosing Sweater Size

Size matters explained

Never did choosing the right size for you seem more complicated! But it is *very* important. After all, you can't try on a sweater that you haven't yet knitted and sizing is pretty tricky when you throw in all the complications of your own personal knitting tension and the fact that once the pieces are knitted, you can't adjust them like you can a sewing pattern piece. Very Pink Knits addresses all that and much, much more, including how to choose a pattern that suits your body shape.

http://youtu.be/apYWysegJfg

KNITTING

Styles and Stitches

English Knitting, Flicking Style

How to never let go

Very Pink Knits explains the way she uses a flicking style to knit English method of knitting. Instead of letting go of the right hand needle, she keeps hold of it and uses a flicking action with her forefinger. This speeds up the work and maintains a better tension. If you're a beginner, you might find this a bit tricky. But, like Very Pink Knits, once you're more practised, you could get fed up of letting go of the needle with every stitch and want to make a conscious decision to change your style. There's no right or wrong with any of the styles – it's really just a matter of what you're comfortable with.

http://youtu.be/y547Q5Hjcuo

English Knitting, Pencil Hold

Another way to hold on

Here's another style of knitting English method – this time, holding the right hand needle like a pencil. Elsteffo explains why she prefers this to a classic flicking style, which only goes to show what any experienced knitter would say: find a style that feels comfortable to you. This tutorial also demonstrates that it's not just the way you hold the needles, but how you hold and tension the yarn that both works for neater knitting and reduces strain in your hands and fingers. Elsteffo doesn't mention it, but some people also like the pencil hold because it supports the weight of the knitting in the V between finger and thumb.

http://youtu.be/ezH4qpn3org

How to Knit Continental Style

Quick knitting the
Continental way

Continental style knitters hold the yarn in their left
hand instead of the right. They position the yarn so
they can pull it through the next loop onto the right
needle in a "picking" fashion, which is why this
method is also called Picking. This tutorial
demonstrates the technique, starting with how
to wind and feed the yarn around your hand and
fingers for even tension. English or Continental style,
the way you choose to knit is up to you: the finished
work will look exactly the same. As you become
more proficient, you might use either, or even both
at the same time, especially if you're knitting two-
colour, such as Fair Isle (see pages 87–95).

http://youtu.be/w9LtDMikq0A

How to Purl Continental Method

How to pick
a purl

Here's how to purl Continental, or by the Picking method. It stands out from other videos on the subject by demonstrating the left finger action very slowly and clearly. This is important because some people can be confused by exactly which way to wrap the yarn round the needle. No confusion here: Cyberseams show both the correct and the incorrect method side by side. In this book, some of the video tutorials use the English Throwing method and others use the Continental Picking method, but don't let that worry you. You'll be able to see exactly what is going on and be able to go ahead and work it in your own individual technique. The end results will be just the same!

http://youtu.be/9VGkXHsY59M

How to Use Circular Needles

Two ways with
one needle

Circular needles aren't just for knitting in the round; you can also use them to knit back and forth. In this video, Catherine Hirst succinctly demonstrates both methods, coming up with useful hints and tips, including a joining method that one experienced knitter commented she'd never seen before. Some garments, such as hats, socks and gloves, have to be knitted in the round but many experienced knitters like to use circular needles even when knitting back and forth because they're neater and easier to handle. Other knitters love to knit all their garments in the round because they hate sewing up at the end.

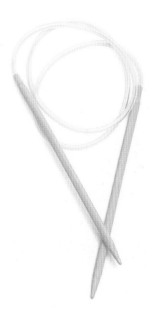

The Magic Loop

What to do when there aren't enough stitches to go round

Circular needles come with different lengths of cable to suit the size of the garment you're knitting. That's great if you're knitting a large garment, but if you want to knit smaller tubes, such as for socks or gloves and the stitches just won't stretch, you need to use the "Magic Loop" method. Liat Gat demonstrates Magic Loop here, both in Continental style knitting and American (another name for English style). It looks fiddly but some people find it easier than using the multiple double pointed needles (dpns) method (see opposite). The end result is the same, whichever type of needle you use.

http://youtu.be/6KccLlkTKzE

Knitting with Double Pointed Needles (dpns)

The traditional solution
to knitting in the round

Knitting in the round was traditionally worked using four or more double pointed needles and it's still a great way to deal with smaller rounds, such as for socks, gloves, and particularly the tiny rounds of glove fingers. All those needles sticking out all over the place can look intimidating if you've never knitted in the round. But Astraknots quickly explains that you're still only working on two needles; the others are there simply to hold the live stitches until you're ready to knit them. She demonstrates the whole process, including a firm crossover method to join the round.

Two by Two Ribbing (k2, p2 Rib)

A popular rib
twosome

For a more defined, stretchy finish, you can use two by two ribbing, which simply means that instead of knitting every alternate stitch in knit and purl, you are working two of each. Ideally, you need a multiple of four stitches to allow for the full pattern repeat but sometimes the pattern doesn't accommodate this neatly. The key is to work knit stitches into knit stitches and purl stitches into purl stitches. This is a very smart and popular rib and well worth learning. Clearly demonstrated here, it explains why and when you need to pass the yarn to the back or the front of the knitting. Repeated several times, the video is easy to follow and understand.

http://youtu.be/R1cRtBpfcwk

Moss (Seed) Stitch

A pretty, easy
background pattern

The knitting action of moss stitch (known as seed stitch in the US) is exactly like ribbing: knit one purl one. The difference, as Catherine Hurst demonstrates, is that in ribbing, you knit where there has been a knit stitch and you purl where there has been a purl stitch; for moss stitch, you do the opposite and knit where there has been a purl stitch and purl where there has been a knit stitch. If that all sounds far too confusing in words, take a look at the video and all will be clear. She also tells us why this is such a useful stitch to have in our basic set of knitting skills.

http://youtu.be/ec2xOVNwINo

Fisherman's Rib

Chunky man-sized ribbing

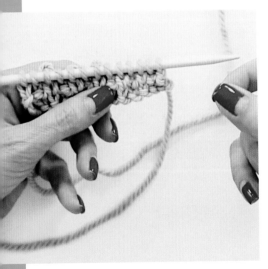

This is a great stitch with a fabulous rich texture that is a whole lot simpler than cable. It knits up into a firm, heavy fabric that looks the same on both sides and is wonderful for scarves and hats. It's easy to do and is much the same as ordinary rib, except there are more knit than purl stitches and at particular points you need to knit into the stitch below. The video shows you exactly how, and, once you've mastered the technique, you'll find you'll create fabric really quickly. As Very Pink Knits says, "This stitch really flies!"

http://youtu.be/02cRYerIVcY

Ricrac Rib

Ribbing in a class
of its own

Really fancy cuffs and welts turn an ordinary sweater into something very special, and this very stretchy rickrack rib is one of Very Pink Knits' favourites. She shows us what it looks like in different weights of yarn, then demonstrates how to work the two row pattern both on straight needles and in the round. Further on in the video, she shows how to cast off while retaining the pattern and stretch. Making up into a firm, flat fabric, this rib would also make a fabulous stitch for scarves and beanie-style hats.

Herringbone Stitch

Tight texture that looks
like it's woven

Herringbone might not be speedy like fisherman's rib, but it does make up into a gorgeous fabric that almost looks as if has been woven. It's a great one to use for scarves, cowls and bags. It is worked over two rows, so you'll need to knit a few rows before you can see the full pattern. As the demonstrator explains, this is not TV knitting. You are going to need to concentrate and keep your eyes on what you're doing, as there's lots of slipping of stitches and you could be in danger of slipping the wrong ones or rather more than you'd planned.

http://youtu.be/1GlQ16pud5A

Loop Stitch

 All fingers and thumbs
for a fun fabric

This loopy stitch is also sometimes called fur stitch, because when it's finished, it does look a bit like a fun fur. As usual, Wool and the Gang use their signature huge wool and needles, but also show a sample of loop stitch in a fine yarn. Loop stitch really is one you need to see demonstrated because the loops are made with the left thumb and transferred to the right thumb, before being knitted in a double action. It is clearly demonstrated several times in this tutorial, and by the end of the row she shows how you can get into a rhythm for speed.

CORRECTING

Errors

Picking Up Dropped Knit Stitches

Dropped stitch
disasters sorted

Sometimes, as you're knitting along, you drop a stitch and you can pick it up before going on to the next. Other times, you drop a stitch and don't realize until later, by which time it's worked down a few rows in the knitting to create a ladder. This video shows you exactly how to put that right using your knitting needles, getting in close to demonstrate which side of the yarn bar the stitch should be on and exactly how to use your needles to restore order to the knitting.

http://youtu.be/1frMR9RUYNl

Fixing a Dropped Purl Stitch

Rescue strategies for
dropped purl stitches

Obvious as it may sound, if you're working on a purl row, you'll need to pick up the stitches purlwise, but it's a problem that stumps many new knitters and tutorials on picking up dropped purl stitches get far more views than their knit equivalent. So take a look! This video shows you how to sort the problem, both with a single dropped stitch and with a ladder using knitting needles. We also see another method of picking up using a crochet hook, which is much easier and niftier. Even if you're not a crochet person, it's worth investing in a crochet hook in your knitting kit specifically for quick fixing.

http://youtu.be/N95rt_g0s9U

Fix Knitting Mistakes by Ripping Stitches

Two ways to rip out
your knitting

Let's get real – hard as it might feel to rip out your knitting, sometimes it has to be done so you can right your wrongs. There are two ways to do this, depending on the situation. If you don't have to pull out very much, you might decide to un-knit the knitting stitch by stitch. This is called "tinking" (the word "knit" backwards!) It is useful, especially if you have a colour or pattern sequence wrong and you just want to take it back to a particular place. Ripping out is much more dramatic, but it might be the quickest solution if there's a fundamental error some rows back. This video demonstrates both tinking and ripping out.

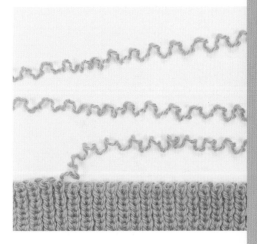

Correctly Mounted versus Twisted Stitches

Twisted stitch remedy: getting
those stitches straight

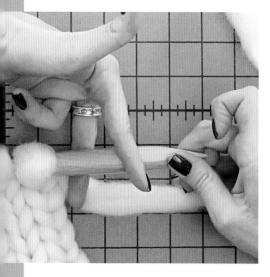

Everyone knows that a knit fabric should have lines of smart, perfectly even little Vs running up and down it. But what if your Vs don't look so smart: if they look just a little twisty? Why has this happened and what should you do about it? If you're a beginner, you might just be knitting into the front, rather than the back of the stitch. Or you may have unravelled a few rows and you've picked them up twisted on your needle. Using massive needles and unspun felting yarn to make easy-to-see mammoth stitches, Very Pink Knits brilliantly demonstrates the problems and their remedies.

http://youtu.be/IbFMKfG_8w8

Lifelines when Ripping Out

Damage limitation when correcting mistakes

So ripping out your knitting looks all fine and dandy when it's a small, perfectly knitted example as in the previous video. But it's not always like that. If you're working with lots of colour or texture, or you have a yarn that occasionally splits, ripping out is not nearly such a smooth affair. Besides, you can sometimes end up ripping out more than you planned and picking up again can be a long and tricky business. Very Pink Knits demonstrates how to put in a lifeline so you can't pull out any more than you want, and you can easily get those stitches back on the needle, all facing in the right direction.

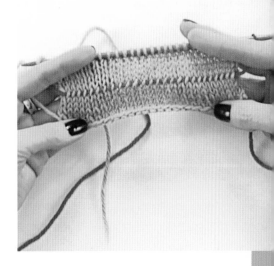

http://youtu.be/ae7pobnLKGQ

SHAPING

Increasing Stitches at Row Ends (kfb and pfb)

Expanding at the edges

To knit shape into garment pieces, you need to increase and decrease stitches. This is often done simply by casting on one or more extra stitches at the beginning of a row. This video demonstrates a much neater way to increase by knitting into the front and back of the stitch (KFB) or purling into the front and back of the stitch (PFB), giving a pretty fashioned edge. This is also called the "bar" method as it leaves a tiny bar just inside the increase.

Make 1 Knitwise (m1k)

Expanding in the
middle of a knit row

Sometimes, you need to increase stitches in the middle of a row, or at equal intervals along the length of it. For example, patterns often specify an increase along the whole row when changing from the ribbed welt of a sweater to the main stocking stitch. This prettily presented video tutorial, shot against a white background, demonstrates clearly how to do this in knit rows.

http://youtu.be/SpbBRF0zm6s

Make 1 Purlwise (m1p)

Expanding in the middle of a purl row

Although knitting pattern instructions usually just instruct us to "Make 1", they don't always specify whether you should do this knitwise or purlwise. It's best to make new stitches in the correct way for purl rows as otherwise they will show up as an error on the right side of the garment. Like most purl stitches, it is a bit trickier to do than its knit equivalent, but in this, the sister video to the one opposite, you can see clearly how it should be worked.

Right Slanting Decreases (k2tog)

Neat decreasing on
the left-hand side

The simplest way to decrease stitches is to knit two together (k2tog) and when this is worked at the end of a knit row, it makes a smart edge along the left hand edge of your work. Elsteffo demonstrates how to do this, making an elegant right slanting edge along the left hand side of the work. She actually demonstrates by decreasing twice at the end of the row, which makes a wider, smarter band, though this is something you should do only if the pattern specifies decreasing two stitches.

http://youtu.be/2hwMZV7Arrc

Left Slanting Decreases (ssk)

Neat decreasing on
the right-hand side

You can decrease on the right hand edge simply by
knitting two together at the beginning of a knit row
but to achieve a smarter finish, you'll need to slip slip
knit (ssk), which is demonstrated here. The two
techniques, demonstrated in this and the previous
video, can also be used in the middle of rows to
make right slanting and left slanting decreases for
three-dimensional shapes – for hats, for example.
You don't need to worry about which technique you
should use when. Knitting patterns are always very
clear as to when you need to use each technique.

http://youtu.be/8gOrRLQn92w

Double Decrease (sl2tog, k1, p2sso)

Taking shape
by taking in

As well as decreasing pieces at the edges, decreasing can also be used to give garments a three-dimensional shape, such as when making a hat. In these situations, you don't always need left or right slanting shaping. Sometimes, you need to create a centred decrease, and this is called a double decrease because the shaping is equal on either side. This shows exactly how to work the double decrease. Patterns usually spell out what you actually need to do, as in "sl2tog p2sso", rather than simply saying "double decrease". So this is more about understanding the technique, rather than committing the terms to memory.

http://youtu.be/en3Yq2er4RI

Short Rows: Wrap and Turn

Turn and turn again:
sophisticated shaping

Most knitting patterns only call for basic increase and decrease techniques. But once you move on to more elaborate shaping, you might find yourself tackling short rows, which means knitting part of the row more than once before moving on. To avoid leaving holes in the work, you need to know how to "wrap and turn". Eunny Jang's tutorial is one of the best on YouTube because she not only shows examples of the finished effect of some wrapping and turning, but demonstrates no less than four different ways of achieving a great finish.

The Art of Sock Making

Socks made simple:
an overview

The idea of making socks can be alarming! There are all sorts of confusing terms, like "heel flap", "short rows" and "toe shaping". If that's not enough to put you off, they're traditionally knitted in the round on fine double pointed needles. Actually, once you get going, they're rather fun to knit: not too big a project and there's plenty going on to keep you interested. This tutorial by Red Heart runs through all the principles, which really helps to get your head around the whole process. Besides, you don't have to knit traditionally fine socks. Think chunky welly boot socks. They'll go much quicker and you can have loads of fun with cables and Fair Isle to turn over the top of your boots.

http://youtu.be/tVkZ85drobs

How to Knit Glove Fingers

Getting your head around
knitting fingers

New knitters might be put off the idea of knitting gloves. Worked in the round with four needles around tiny little glove fingers, there are times when the work looks more like a game of pick-up-sticks than knitting. But if you're a comfortable knitter, don't be put off. Girly Knits shows you step by step how to deal with the digits. Like socks, they're a quick knit project compared to a sweater and now that fingerless gloves have become quite the fashion accessory, once you get going, you can have real fun with fancy colours and stitches.

http://youtu.be/EjrCR9FDAuQ

Making Mitred Squares

Perfect squares: a knitting
building block

Knowing how to knit perfect mitred squares is handy for many reasons. They have sharp corners and when knitted in garter stitch, they lie flat and so can be used in many different ways such as for coasters, mats or dish cloths. You can also knit up loads to stitch together into a blanket, for example, using different yarn colours and taking advantage of the stitch directions to make up interesting designs. To make mitres, you cast on two sides of a square, then use increases and decreases to form the shape until you get down to just one stitch and your perfect square! VeryPink Knits shows you how.

http://youtu.be/ZHxabZA-dGk

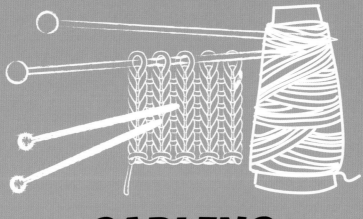

CABLING

Reading Charts

The back and forth of understanding charts

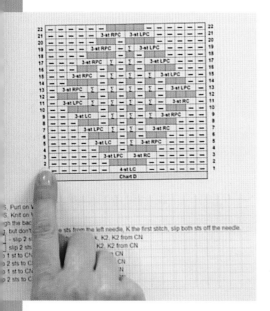

Any pattern that has a repeat design, whether it's a cable or lace pattern, or a colour design, is likely to include a chart, which is a diagrammatic layout of the design. Sometimes, there may even be two or more charts, each one representing a different part of the design. In this video, Very Pink Knits demonstrates the basic principles of using both texture and colour charts, and explains how to read them when you're knitting back and forth and how to read them when you're knitting in the round. It's a simple and useful overview. There are more detailed tutorials later on reading cable charts (see opposite) and lace charts (see page 74).

http://youtu.be/LJBO6PzQeTc

Reading a Cable Chart

Understanding cable
chart symbols

Not all patterns for cable knits have a chart. They
simply give instructions for when to purl, when to
knit and when to cable to the front or back etc. But
some patterns do have charts and these can be so
confusing for some people that they write out the
pattern in full before embarking on the knitting.
But others prefer charts once they understand the
symbols. For them, it's easier to knit along checking
the diagram as they go, rather than finding the right
part of the pattern to check the instructions. This
tutorial explains the symbols, using a chart to show
you what you should be doing and when.

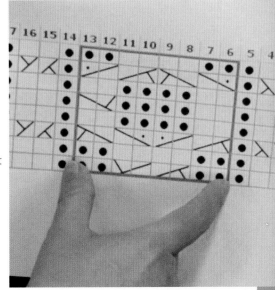

An Introduction to Knitting Cables

Understanding cables:
the big picture

Learn to cable and you'll have the key to a treasure chest of wonderful knitted textures and patterns, including many that date back to ancient Celtic days. The basic principle comes down to changing the order in which you knit the stitches off the left hand needle so that the cables appear to twist out of the body of the fabric. This video demonstrates this very clearly using a design that incorporates both a right twisting cable and left twisting cable and showing how they can look different, depending on how many rows you work into the design. The different kinds of cable needles are also demonstrated, with information on what size to choose and how to use them.

http://youtu.be/_HgPp6Y8_ME

Working a Front Cable (c4f)

Learning to
do the twist

Cables can be used in combination to make up endless designs, some of which date back to ancient Saxon and Celtic times. When cabling, you place the stitches held on a cable needle to the front or the back of the work, depending on which direction you want the cable to twist. Pattern instructions will tell you exactly which you should do. The letter "c" indicates you are going to cable. The number (in this case 4) tells you how many stitches to put on the needle. The letter "f" means you hold the stitches to the front. The letter "b" means you hold the stitches to the back. This video demonstrates c4f.

Right and Left Twisted Stitches (c1f and c1b)

A neat solution for travelling stitches

At its simplest, a single cable stitch makes "travelling" or "twisted" stiches, which you can use to make patterns such as a trellis, diagonal textures or tiny cable twists. They are worked in exactly the same way as any other cabling by holding one stitch to the front or the back of the work. Some people find this a little fiddly and there is a danger the stitch will slip off the cable needle (depending what kind of cable needle you are using). Here is a nifty alternative way to work travelling stitches without using a cable needle.

http://youtu.be/jS5HMe3GIYk

Making Bobbles (mb)

A masterclass on
making bobbles

Bobbles are very much part of the cable tradition
and can be used decoratively throughout a pattern
either singly or in grape-like groups. They're not
difficult to make and use up only one stitch so there's
no complicated pattern to remember. It all comes
down to making loads of stitches into one stitch,
knitting a couple of rows on these few stitches, then
casting them off again so you're left with just one
stitch before you carry on knitting the row.
Demonstrating using easy-to-see large needles
and yarn, Pleasant Seas shows you how!

The Story of the Aran Sweater

The mysteries and meanings
of ancient Aran knitting

OK, so this isn't a tutorial but it is a rather beautiful explanation of the history of Aran sweaters, told from the Aran islands off the west coast of Ireland where the designs evolved around the lives and environment of an ancient people. It explains the relevance and meanings of the patterns and how and why they evolved over the centuries to the present day. Many of the designs echo ancient Celtic art that is still found on old stones, crosses and even jewellery. It's a fascinating story that gives meaning to our knitting today.

http://youtu.be/rDDE-ZwCaZo

Saxon Braid

 A pretty pattern using
cable techniques

Once you know how to cable, there is no end to the
wonderful textures you can create. This pretty Saxon
braid is an example where the stitches travel and
interweave, rather than cable in a rope-like fashion.
Pleasant Seas shows very clearly how to create
the pattern, explaining as she goes. The relevant
instructions are also written out on the video, which
both helps beginners to understand how to read
cable patterns and gives a quick reference for
experienced knitters. This pattern can be
incorporated into any stocking stitch sweater,
though it could affect the tension, so make sure you
include it in full on your tension square before
beginning to knit the garment.

http://youtu.be/LV5c-PSAeiE

LACE
Knitting

Yarn Over (yo)

The easy foundation
for lace knitting

For lacy patterns, you need to be able to make holes in your work and the main skill you'll need is "yarn over". Elsteffo shows how to do this both on the knit side and the purl side, explaining that this will form an increase in stitches. On its own, yarn over can be used where increases are needed with the added interest of lace detailing. If you don't want to make increases, you'll need to then decrease a stitch, which you can do either by knitting two together or slipping a stitch over. The pattern will tell you which is the best for the design.

http://youtu.be/ol4rbwC3dql

Yarn Round Needle Twice

Big holes for double
the drama

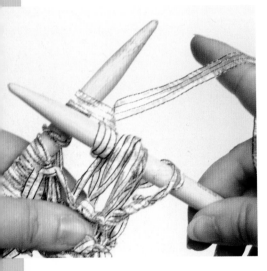

To make really large holes, the pattern sometimes tells us us to wrap the yarn around the needle several times. This can be used in fine lace knitting, or, for a more dramatic effect, with fancy yarns, such as this pretty striped ribbon yarn. This video shows you how to master the technique in words and still pictures, including how you knit the next row to avoid increasing the stitches on your needle. It all looks a little confusing until you come to the end of the purl row, when the pattern begins to take shape.

http://youtu.be/vw0tCwkA4YQ

Triple Yarn Over

A speedy solution for quick knitting

This video shows you what a triple yarn over looks like when worked on very large needles with very thick yarn. Try this for a scarf and you'll have a long, lacy one knitted in no time. Again, what you seem to be doing is making three stitches for every one you knit, but as you slip them all off again as you purl, by the end of the row, you're left with the original amount of stitches you cast on. As they demonstrate this technique, Wool and the Gang reassure us that dropping all those stitches might be counterintuitive, but it will result in a great finished project!

http://youtu.be/HsPKt2Bh_cs

Yarn Over with Slip Slip Knit (yo, ssk)

Increasing and decreasing to
make lace patterns: version 1

Once you're confident knitting and purling, most knitting techniques are pretty straightforward. It can be deciphering the pattern instruction that is not so straightforward. You just need someone to show you exactly where to put that needle and how to slip it over! This video is a real case in point. Iknitwithcatfur is a real mistress of technique and has a straight-forward way of delivering. In this video, she demonstrates two ways to work the yarn over slip slip knit stitch and divulges her way to get it really neat. Now that's neat!

http://youtu.be/RSZFpoBqDpo

Yarn Over Knit Two Together (yo, k2tog)

Foundation lace stitch:
version 2

This is much easier to understand than the yo ssk, but the principle is the same: you are reducing the stitches you added in the last row as you made a yarn over to create the hole in the fabric. So the knitting should stay the same width. The pattern will tell you which stitch you should use to counteract the yarn over. Depending on the situation, the finished effects will be different. So don't take short cuts, follow the instructions! Judy shows you how to do yo k2tog. She says it's simple and it really is. It is so deceptively simple that beginners can overcomplicate it, so it's great to see exactly how the experts do it.

How to Follow a Lace Knitting Chart Knitwise

Mastering the art of reading
lace chart – knitwise

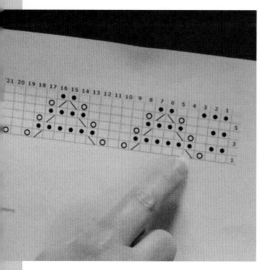

Just like cable designs, lace knitting patterns sometimes come with a chart to show you when to yarn over, slip slip knit or knit two together. It's a little more complicated than the cable equivalent in that the very nature of lace knitting is adding and subtracting stitches while keeping to the same amount of stitches across the row. So, for example, slip slip knit involves two stitches, but it is only one action so gets one box on the chart. It does take a bit of getting your head around, so Planet Purl takes her time and carries out the tutorial over two videos.

http://youtu.be/n_8I7IvpA8U

How to Follow a Lace Knitting Chart Purlwise

The opposite way to decipher the symbols

The tricky part of following lace pattern charts is that for each symbol on the legend, it means one stitch on the knit side but the opposite one on the purl side. This is more complicated than a colour chart, for example, because a colour is a colour, whichever side you're working on. Beth Moriarty clears up any confusion as she shows and tells how she knits along the first purl row. As we can see the knitting growing and stitch pattern appearing she shows us how the chart is really a preview of the design, and once you get going, you can anticipate the next stage of the stitch pattern.

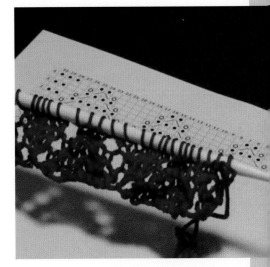

Using Lifelines with Lace Knitting

The lace knitting
safety belt

Noticing a mistake way back and having to rip out your knitting is never a good feeling. It's even more annoying if you've been working an intricate lace pattern, firstly because the last thing you want is to overshoot and secondly because picking up stitches that have been yarned over, slip stitched and knitted together is something of a challenge. This tutorial shows you how to take the strain from the problem, by putting in lifelines. For lace knitting, you do need to put in lifelines at regular intervals as you knit. But that means if you need to, you can safely unravel and quickly pick up the stitches again.

http://youtu.be/elJqui-bM-k

Belgian Lace Edging

The prettiest trim
from a bygone era

Thumbing her way through old publications, Iknitwithcatfur digs out some utterly charming combinations, which she shares on a weekly basis. This delightful lace edging dates back to a copy of the *New York Tribune* in the late 1800s and can be used as a trim for any fine knitting such as a baby's shawl or bonnet. It has an 11-stitch pattern repeat and is worked over eight rows. If you want to use it as an edging, knit up all the garment pieces, then knit up the length of edging you'll need for each piece. Stitch it in place using neat mattress stitch (see page 103).

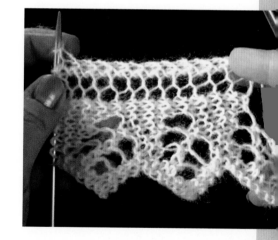

How to Block Lace Knitting

Shaping up your lace knitting

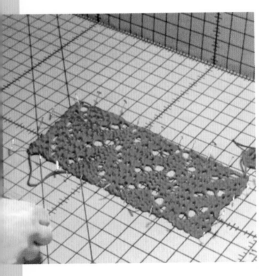

All knitted pattern pieces should be blocked (flattened and pulled into shape) before you sew them together and there's another tutorial on that (see page 102). But the very laciness of lace knitting needs extra special care and this video demonstrates all the steps you need to take to encourage what often starts out as a scrappy-looking piece of knitting into its full, even-stitched glory. Although Planet Purl uses a purpose-designed blocking board and special pins, you can achieve the same effect using ordinary folded bath towels as a base and long dressmaking pins.

http://youtu.be/ub-3IVbQt64

COLOUR WORK

– Stripes and Intarsia

Adding a New Colour to Your Knitting

A neat solution
for adding yarns

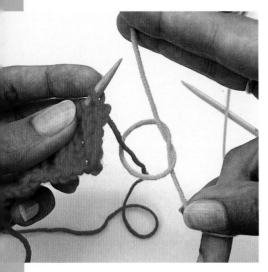

There are many ways to knit with colour, the simplest of which is to knit in stripes. The other two main methods are Fair Isle, where you interweave (usually two) colours along the row as you go along, and intarsia, which is made up of blocks of colour that can be used to create elaborate designs such as repeat motifs, logos and pictures. Tutorials on all these are reviewed later in the book. But essentially, whatever method you use, you will need to attach new colours at certain points in the knitting. This video shows you how.

http://youtu.be/eyeoyY1T9U4

Carrying Colours for Stripes

Neat edges for
stripey work

Stripes might be simple, but they are very effective, even if you decide just to knit striped ribbing set against a mainly plain sweater. You can keep adding in the colour as you need it, but that would leave loads of loose ends to be woven in when you've finished knitting the piece. This tutorial shows how to neatly carry the colours over without affecting the tension (and therefore the shape of the piece). As Very Pink Knits points out, this only works if each colour is used for an even number of rows so the "spare" colour can be taken up the sides of the piece. A simple, but effective technique.

Intarsia Knitting – The Basics

Getting the picture: knitting
motifs into your work

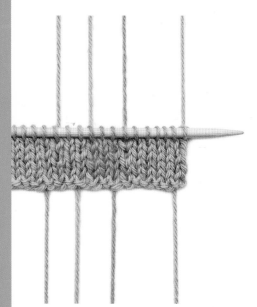

Using big wool and needles, Wool and the Gang
introduce this video by demonstrating the difference
between Fair Isle and intarsia knitting. They then go
on to show in detail how to knit intarsia, twisting the
yarns together at the back to avoid leaving any holes
in the work, and managing the many balls of yarn,
which they admit do get somewhat tangled as you
knit, especially with all that twisting. London fashion
designers with a passion for knitting, Wool and the
Gang are like a breath of fresh air on the knitting
scene with their quest to encourage men and young
knitters to get out their needles and get knitting.

http://youtu.be/hR0rJyl-COQ

Colour Work and Managing Yarns

 Ways to untangle the multiple yarn problem

Knitters are constantly exchanging ideas as to how to knit with several different colours without getting into a tangle. In this video, Eunny Jang takes an overview of several different ways to manage the various coloured yarns both for Fair Isle knitting (or "stranded", which is another name for it) and intarsia. The Fair Isle section is slightly confused because she's knitting in the round with double pointed needles, but that's when managing the colours deftly becomes even more important, especially when working on the smallest sections such as the fingers of gloves.

Yarn Butterflies and Yarn Bobbins

Keeping order the
traditional way

One of the most convenient ways to manage colours, which is not mentioned in many videos, is to use yarn bobbins, which are available online and from knitting shops. They come in several shapes, but some of the best are small fish-shaped ones with a tiny slit at the head end to feed the yarn through. This video shows yarn bobbin variations on the same theme. You make up a bobbin for each colour, and as you become more practised, you'll find you can easily flick from one to another, as you twist the colours together without getting the yarn tangled. This video also shows make-your-own cardboard alternatives and how to wind bobbin-free yarn butterflies.

http://youtu.be/jabwPfJZxto

Weaving in the Loose Ends

A neat finish for
colour work

When knitting intarsia, you will be left with loads of
loose ends, and these need to be woven in before
you block the pieces and stitch them together. In
this tutorial, Chemknits demonstrates how to weave
in those ends so that they don't show at the front
of the work and do not easily unravel. She also
demonstrates how to fix any small holes where the
colours meet as you weave in the ends. It's clearly so
well presented that nobody has any doubts as to
how to weave in. Of the 40,000 views, there are only
four comments!

http://youtu.be/Pva0lc7qXlE

Linen Stitch

Easy-to-knit,
two-colour pattern

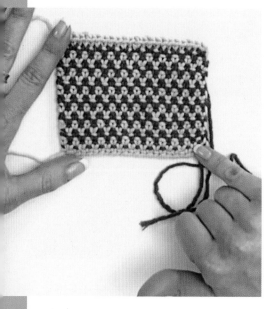

Firm, flat and more like a woven fabric than knitting, this stitch is great for anything such as mats or a scarf that you don't want to curl up like stocking stitch. When you work it in two colours, you get a fantastic pattern that really does look like a sophisticated textile weave. Yet it really is not difficult to do. It's just a knit/purl two row repeat, much like stocking stitch except you slip every other stitch. As well as demonstrating exactly how to work this (do watch, Very Pink Knits also explains which side of the work the yarn needs to be on), the written instructions are given on her website in pdf form.

http://youtu.be/6o0Y4Yu6wuA

FAIR ISLE

Colour Knitting

The Fair Isle Chart

Keeping track of
intricate designs

The pretty, traditional Scandinavian and Fair Isle designs can look very complicated, but armed with the chart provided on all Fair Isle knitting patterns, they are not difficult to master. For a general overview on reading any chart, see page 60. Many Fair Isle sweater patterns include more than one chart as different design motifs are used in different parts of the overall design. This tutorial gives hints and tips on how to keep track of where you are. In practice, depending on how complicated the pattern is, once you've completed several repeats, it's not difficult to keep track by watching the shapes as they grow.

http://youtu.be/pZd8Kq6N8c8

Fair Isle Knitting – Basic Techniques

The key to ancient colour design

Using a simple two-colour herringbone design, Alexis Winslow demonstrates the Fair Isle technique using the English knitting method. It's a great video for beginners to understand as it is easy to see what is going on without being distracted by the often-complicated traditional designs or by any particular knitting style. Most Fair Isle designs are worked in no more than two colours per row, and the colour not in use is carried across as a "float" at the back of the work. As Alexis points out, everyone has their own way of managing the yarns. She demonstrates hers, where she holds both colours in one hand, feeding in each yarn as it is needed.

http://youtu.be/QeAIkNltWz8

Fair Isle Knitting Holding One Yarn in Each Hand

The ambidextrous way
to keep yarns in order

Many experienced knitters find it easiest to work Fair Isle holding one colour in each hand, and then knitting Continental method with the left hand and English method using the right. Although this was touched on in Eunny's tutorial on page 83, this video is much clearer, allowing more time to go into a lot more detail. Also, very cleverly, there is a link to both methods that you can click as you watch the video. As well as the basic technique, Kyoko shows us how to keep an even tension.

http://youtu.be/JOYBE11s640

Three Colour Stranding

Smart management
of three colours

Most Fair Isle knitting keeps to two colours in one
row but some Scandinavian, and particularly
Icelandic, designs use three or more colours in a row.
In this video, Knitpicks demonstrates how to manage
this, which she does neatly using a combination of
Continental and English knitting styles, holding two
of the colours in her right hand. Using three colours,
these traditional designs are rich and attractive, but
also, as all the yarn travels across the back of the
work, the sweaters are extremely thick and warm,
designed to withstand the coldest of winters.

http://youtu.be/vEzWdMlKj_Q

Fair Isle Knitting in the Round

The hows and whys of
working in the round

By knitting Fair Isle in the round, you never have to purl and you can follow each round on the chart from right to left. Many people find this easier than using straight needles, and they're joining a time-honoured tradition as in times gone by, Fair Isle knitting was generally done in the round so no shaping or sewing up was needed. Where openings were needed, they cut steeks (see opposite). You can use circular or double pointed needles (see pages 33 and 35). This tutorial by Patons shows exactly how to master the technique in clear, easy steps.

http://youtu.be/OyvLlg2lXsM

Understanding Steeks

Why you sometimes need
to cut up your work

The most scary thing you could ask a knitter to do is
to take the scissors to their work. But cutting a steek
is one of the classic techniques of making Fair Isle
sweaters. Traditionally, Fair Isle and Norwegian
sweaters are knitted in the round to avoid purling
and ensure the pattern matches at the edges. So you
finish up with a huge tube and you then need to
make cuts for the sleeves and any other opening.
Paula Fuessie demonstrates the principles on her
fabulous newly stitched Norwegian sweater. She's
prepared the steek so we can watch as she takes a
huge pair of scissors to her work.

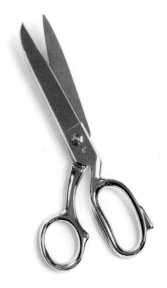

http://youtu.be/rJgTFGvKmgQ

Steeks Step by Step

Scissoring the steeks
the non-scary way

No apologies for two videos on steeks. Paula's gives a great overview offering an excellent general understanding, but in this tutorial, Kerin really gets down to the nitty gritty, showing us how wide to knit the steek, what patterns to use and how to prepare them by hand. She is clearly experienced at this and, rather than finding it scary, sees steeking as an exciting moment. She explains why steeking works well using natural animal fibres such as wool and gives tips as to how you can make allowances if you are using other fibres such as cotton. Finally, the scissors she takes to the knitting are extremely sharp but extremely small … and she explains why.

http://youtu.be/buKv6Wg8TcY

Swedish Weave

Clever woven-in colour

Here's a pretty way to add colour to your work without the complications of Fair Isle or Intarsia. Technically, you are not knitting your detail colour – you're just weaving it back and forth between the needles. Iknitwithcatfur is an extremely proficient knitter and delivers in an easy-to-understand way, bringing plenty of detail on how to keep the tension even and how to cast off. Knitting Continental style, she observes that it is quite fiddly. People used to knitting Fair Isle holding one yarn in each hand (see page 90) might find this a quicker, less fiddly way to work.

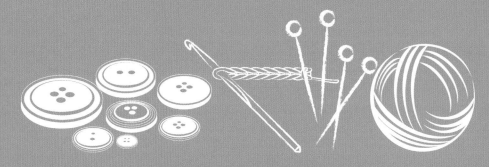

FINISHING

and Care

Pick Up and Knit

Horizontal and vertical grafting on

When you're knitting garments, you often need to pick up and knit stitches from finished, cast-off pieces. This will be, for example, if you want to add a button band or any other kind of edging. In this video, Knit Purl Hunter demonstrates how to pick up and knit along a horizontal edge and then how to pick up and knit down a vertical edge, explaining why you need to pick up fewer stitches on the vertical than you do across the horizontal. She uses coloured markers to highlight the relevant stitches and contrast yarn for the picking up and knitting, so all is clear.

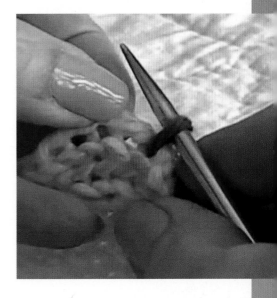

Pick Up Stitches around a Neck Edge

Grafting on around
a neckline

Picking up and knitting stitches around a neck edge is not so straightforward as you have horizontal sections and decreased sections that are not quite vertical. But since the neck edge is a focal point, the finish is key. Cheryl Brunette shows you exactly how to tackle each part, and then how to neatly finish off the neckband. This is extremely useful as patterns can be vague, telling us, for example, to "pick up and knit evenly around the neckline". Armed with the information from this tutorial, it will be much easier to know exactly where you should pick up for each stitch.

http://youtu.be/tV5UQ-W8WMQ

How to Graft Live Stitches to a Cast-On Edge

The neatest join
in the round

If you want to seam knitting sideways, such as to join the ends of a cowl or hand warmers, instead of casting off at the end, you can graft the live stitches onto the edge you cast on at the beginning of the project. Kirsten Hipsky demonstrates how to do this using yarn and a darning needle. She replicates the knit stitches so that you really can't see the join. This is also a useful technique if you are knitting something like a contemporary-style sweater where a horizontal piece of knitting needs to be grafted onto a vertical piece.

One Stitch Buttonholes

Buttonholes the quick
and easy way

While dressmakers dread buttonholes, knitters have little to worry about. At its most simple, you're just making a deliberate hole in the work and this affects only one row. Wool and the Gang show you how to do this both on a knit row and a purl row, demonstrating with their signature huge yarn and needles. This does have its limitations in that the button size is limited by the gauge of the knitting – so don't expect to be able to add design details such as big buttons on a fine-knit cardigan.

http://youtu.be/cmRDRXxkI-A

One Row Buttonholes

 A tailored finish for any
size of buttonhole

For rather more tailored buttonholes, you'll need to knit to the relevant position, then, do some casting off, casting on and reinforcing of both ends before continuing the row. It's not difficult. You just need to work through step by step and Amy shows you exactly how, throwing in hints and tips to keep the tension even throughout for a smart finish. This is a useful video to bookmark because, while most knitting patterns explain how to work the button-holes for that particular design, not all do. This tutorial could save the day!

Blocking

 Getting the knitting
into shape

Newly cast off pieces of knitting have a habit of looking like they've just come out of the dog basket. The edges are curly, some of the stitches don't look so even and they can look a little mis-shapen. That's where blocking comes in. By wetting or steaming the pieces and pinning them out, the project really starts to take shape and the stitches look a whole lot better. To the uninitiated, blocking is a mystery process requiring all kinds of special equipment. This video tutorial removes the mystery: Kristen demonstrates the technique using a bowl of water, an old beach towel and some pins.

http://youtu.be/cmyuX3q4ch8

Sewing Up: Mattress Stitch

Two ways to sweater
seam perfection

Once all the pieces are blocked, you're ready
to get stitching them together. Cheryl Brunette
demonstrates two invisible ways to join the seams:
one for when you're stitching the rib sections
together and the other for the main bulk of stocking
stitch. Both are variations of mattress stitch, which is
the classic way to seam hand knit sweaters. Cheryl
has great authority in the way she delivers and she
always demonstrates on fabulous whole garments,
sewing up in "real time", which is rather more
reassuring than on swatches or mini samples.

How to Seam Garter Stitch

The neat, invisible way
to join garter knitting

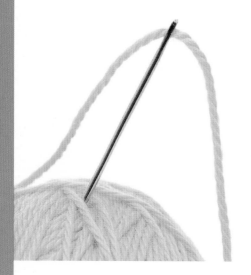

The bumpy lines created by garter stitch demands a different seam than the mattress stitch used for stocking stitch. This video explains exactly how to seam garter stitch neatly and invisibly, throwing in tips as to how to make sure the end result is flat and not cinched in at any point. Using a large darning needle, it is very clear exactly where on the knit stitch it should be inserted. Demonstrated in contrast yarn, it is easy to follow throughout, right up to when it is firmly finished off at the end.

http://youtu.be/Sl0o_k3jYO4

Setting In Sleeves

The smooth way
to sew in sleeves

Badly set in sleeves ruin even the most beautifully knitted sweaters. As Very Pink Knits observes, this is the most difficult part of sewing together a sweater because, unlike at the side seams, the pieces don't match row for row. There are increases and decreases, curves and diagonals to take into account. Shot straight overhead so that you can see how the pieces fit together, we are shown how to start by marking the sleeve to make sure it fits perfectly into the correct position in the armhole. She also tells us how to coax the pieces together and where to take in any extra bulk.

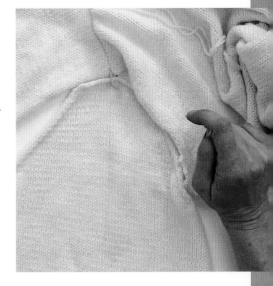

Kitchener Stitch

The neat way to stitch invisible seams

Sometimes, you need to create a neat, flat, invisible seam, at the toe end of socks, for example, because a normal ridgy seam would be most uncomfortable. Kitchener stitch is the traditional way to do this. It mimics the knit stitch and is created by using a darning needle to weave in and out of the stitches. This video shows us exactly how to do this, using contrast yarn for clarity. You work in pairs of stitches that are still on the needle and it can be difficult to remember whether you should be putting the sewing needle in knitwise or purlwise, so we're given a handy little chant to help us remember. Might not be so catchy, but it works!

http://youtu.be/jEXYKxmD_T8

Washing Hand Knits

Gentle care for pure
wool hand knits

Unless they are laundered and dried properly, wool
garments will become matted, misshapen or even
shrink to such an extent you won't be able to wear
them again. Disaster enough with a bought garment:
heart-breaking if you've spent many a long evening
knitting a masterpiece. But cared for properly by
hand washing, hand knitted garments can look
forward to a long and beautiful life. In this video, the
whole procedure is demonstrated from the choice of
soap to use, the temperature of the water, squeezing
techniques and easing the garments into shape
before drying.

DECORATIVE DETAILS

and Projects

Making a Fringe

A pretty, easy way
to add interest

Fringes look great at the ends of scarves, edges of cushion covers, or, if you have a bit of a hippy streak, at the hems of cardigans and boleros. Camille starts off by winding yarn around a book to create identical lengths of fringing, and then demonstrates how to attach them to the end of a scarf using a crochet hook. She finishes off with signature double knots for style. Working with chunky yellow fringing onto a chunky indigo garter-knitted scarf, it all looks very quick, easy and very beginner-do-able.

Double and Triple Knotted Fringes

Classic ways to get
clever with fringing

Fringes made with at least four strands of yarn can be divided, re-divided and knotted as many times as you like to make a more elaborate vintage-style trims for shawls and blankets. Iknitwithcatfur explains that you will need to cut the original fringe longer than if you were making standard fringing, then demonstrates how to make the knots. She doesn't explain how to get the knots even along the horizontal lines, leaving us to work it out for ourselves by adjusting the knots once they're all made.

http://youtu.be/OMEUVNVeWrY

Making Tassels

A whizzy way to create
classic trimmings

Woah! Libbie Summers doesn't hang around! It takes just fifteen seconds for her to demonstrate all you need to know about making tassels using just yarn and a pair of scissors. She makes hers by wrapping yarn around her hand; if you'd prefer bigger or smaller tassels just cut a piece of card to size and away you go! Tassels use more yarn than you might expect, so if you decide to add some to your project, make one to size in scrap yarn, then calculate how much extra you need to buy. Tassels look great trimming hats, scarves and the corners of cushions.

Making Pompoms

Fun trimmings for hats

Classic beanies are topped with pompoms – another trim that works well with knitting that is so easy and fun to do that the kids will want to help. You can make your own round template from cardboard, then all you need is the yarn and some scissors and away you go. This video shows you exactly how to make the template using items from around the house, then demonstrates how to make a pompom and how to stitch it onto a hat. Handily, it also tells you exactly how much yarn you'll need to make a bobble of a certain size, so you'll know how much extra yarn you'll need to buy.

http://youtu.be/c2gQ7spESLg

How to Knit an I-cord

Knitting in the round on two needles

I-cords are knitted cords that can be used in many different ways: as ties, drawstrings or laces for fastenings, for example. Or you can knit up a short i-cord on the top of a beanie hat to create a cute pixie look. This tutorial shows how easy, fun and quick i-cords are to knit. They turn out as tiny tubes that you can knit as long as you want. Although they are technically knitted in the round, this video shows how they are worked on just two double pointed needles.

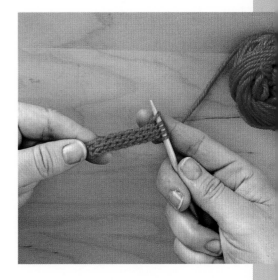

Swiss Darning or Duplicate Stitch

How to sew the
knit stitch

Sometimes there are tiny motifs – or even single stitches - incorporated into intarsia designs. These are far easier to sew in by hand than to work into the design with knitted stitches. The traditional way is to use a duplicate stitch – so called because it is hand stitched on top of the knitting using a darning needle. This technique is also called Swiss darning. It is not difficult and this tutorial shows exactly how to work it, starting with which sewing needles to use. Although this video shows the motif being sewn onto knitting that is still on the needle, Swiss darning is usually stitched on once the knitted pieces are complete and cast off.

http://youtu.be/Afk--2mS7rc

Knitting with Beads: Stringing Method

Knit-along
embellishment

Beads add pattern, sparkle and weight, making garments look gorgeous! Stringing them is the classic way to knit them in and here's how to do it. Knitpicks explains you need to string the beads onto the yarn before you start knitting so you can feed them in where they are needed. The one problem that most people encounter is: how many beads for your ball of yarn? The answer is that unless you can calculate it accurately and easily, don't bother. Guess! When you run out of beads, just break the yarn, string on some more, re-attach the yarn to your knitting and away you go.

Knitting with Beads: Hook Method

Hooking up
with beads

If you're deft with a crochet hook, this method might suit you. You'll need the smallest crochet hook available because it has to be able to fit inside the hole of the bead and then pull two thicknesses of yarn through, ready to be knitted. The advantage this method has over the stringing method is that there's no guesswork involved. You just pick up the beads as you need them and hook a loop of yarn through ready for knitting. With the fine yarn and small beads that are being used to demonstrate, this does look very fiddly. But it might be brilliant with big beads and chunky yarns.

http://youtu.be/3Nrgyqwg2Lw

How to Finger Knit a Necklace

Making a necklace with
your fingers and thumbs

This has to be the coolest finger-knitting tutorial on
the planet! London Central St Martins art student
Kasia Franczak clearly demonstrates how to finger
knit as she makes a fabulous Nefertiti necklace
named after the beautiful ancient Egyptian queen.
Kasia takes us through casting on, finger knitting
and casting off. The technique is easy, fun and
produces great results, so it's a perfect way to
introduce kids to knitting. But don't let the kids
have all the fun – this necklace, made in a fabulous
combination of lemon yellow and striped black yarn
cut from T-shirt material, just oozes cool.

How to Arm Knit an Infinity Scarf

Getting up to your
elbows in knitting

For quick and easy results, arm knitting is the way to go. In less than twenty minutes, Maggie shows us how to knit an infinity scarf or cowl (if you watch to the end of the video, you'll see there's a bit of a discussion about exactly what it is, but it's fast, it's pretty and that's all that matters). This is as much a tutorial as a DIY project as Maggie shows us everything we need to know about arm knitting. It's a great technique that children would love. PS: we love the doggy bloopers at the end!

http://youtu.be/7MMaw_TTxkY

Fingerless Gloves

Cute handwarmers knitted in no time

Here's a cute pair of knit-in-no-time fingerless gloves. As long as you can knit and purl, you can do this as there are no tricksy stitches and there's no shaping – just ribbing and stocking stitch with a bit of sewing up at the end. It's a great first project as it's quick, fun and you can knit and wear all in the same day. As the tutorial says, it's not so much about the knitting – more about "looking right". Once you've got the knack, you can practise your cabling, Fair Isle and fancy stitch skills while making loads of pairs – one for every outfit.

How to Knit a Big Hat

Easiest ever beanie
for beginners

If you can cast on, knit, purl and decrease, you'll easily be able to knit this hat. Running to two videos, this tutorial really does take you step by step from making the first slipstitch to sewing on the pompom at the end. Sheep and Stitch teaches us how to cast on, rib, knit stocking stitch, decrease and use double pointed needles. The first video provides a link to the second one. Beautifully presented as a knit along, Sheep and Stitch takes you through step by step in such fine detail, you could probably manage to knit this hat even if you're a complete beginner.

http://youtu.be/23gmF0WFXdI

Easy Baby Hat

Easy beanie,
pixie style

This cute pixie hat is great both for baby boys and baby girls and it really is easy to master with full instructions for newborn to twelve months. Knitted in the round in k2 p2 rib, it's just a matter of casting on, knitting for the specified length and then decreasing as instructed and finishing with an i-cord for the top. All the instructions are written on the video to go with the voiceover. And just in case you can't catch all that, there's a Ravelry address for downloading the free pattern.

http://youtu.be/urTrn-OpZhg

Chunky Cabled Cowl

Knit-in-an-hour
cabled cowl

In four and a half minutes, Stefanie Japel demonstrates how to knit a chunky cabled cowl in an hour. She tells us how many stitches to cast onto a circular needle, but doesn't let us know what yarn to use. It looks like two strands of double knitting, producing a wonderful chunky knit that would keep out draughts on the coldest winter's day. Stefanie demonstrates the cables without using cable needles, which, especially as she is using large needles, is definitely do-able, but there's nothing to stop you using a cable needle if that would make you feel more comfortable. If you want to learn and practice cabling, this is a great quickie project to get you going.

http://youtu.be/kV-JFskieSE

Country Cottage Pillow Cover

Knit your own soft
furnishings

It's the pretty textured pattern and decorative looped edging that gives this delightful cottage cushion cover its charm. And while there's no shaping to worry about when it comes to cushion covers, those wonderful stitch patterns might stump beginner knitters. But doyenne of lace stitches iknitwithcatfur clearly demonstrates both the stitch pattern for the cushion front and the lovely loopy cast off edge. It's all quite fiddly, so it's not going to be a whizzy TV knit – but then, compared to a sweater, there's not a huge amount of knitting. There's also a free pdf of the pattern.

http://youtu.be/LRqJ9lbgNhs

Summer Beach Bag

Pretty but practical: the great summer tote

Whether you're heading for the beach or off to a festival, you'll want to use this wonderful hippy-inspired bag all summer long. The smart diagonal stitch pattern not only looks pretty; it also adds strength to the bag. Knitted in soft ecru cotton, it should wash like a dream (though check the care label to be sure). This is one of a few rare genuinely one-stop free knitting projects on YouTube. All the instructions are put up on the tutorial as Pleasant Seas demonstrates how to knit the bag, and just in case you missed or didn't understand anything, you'll find them written out in the box below the video.

http://youtu.be/gxmaXZgR-c4

Bumblebee and Ladybird Baby Hats

Cute bug hats
for babies

Cute, fun and so quick to knit on two needles, you'll be making ladybird and bumblebee hats for every new baby in the family. And if you (or the mum) don't like bugs, then you can always make one up in a pretty plain colour. This is one of Pleasant Seas' hat of the month tutorials, most of which are Disney inspired. Pleasant Seas demonstrates how to knit the hats clearly and simply, throwing in tips for tension and technique. Instructions come up on the video to accompany the voiceover and they're also printed out in full below the video.

Tassel Hat

Easy-knit hat for
boys and girls

This is the easiest ever hat to knit, with no shaping to worry about, but it's a brilliant project for a new knitter as there are loads of skills to learn: working in the round, ribbing and knitting in stripes. You'll also be able to practise a three needle cast off (bind off) and end up with making tassels to trim. Very Pink Knits really does show you the whole process step by step, giving herself enough time to do this by dividing the tutorial over four videos. Once you've learned the process, it will be easy to simply increase the number of stitches and knit extra rows to make hats for older girls and boys!

http://youtu.be/N5FyIYvPQyc

Striped Herringbone Scarf

Winter never looked so good:
three gorgeous scarves

Knit yourself an enviable scarf or cowl, plain or striped, with or without pompom – all from this one free pattern. But the winning part of this is that Castingoncouch has worked out a simpler than usual, easy to work herringbone stitch that also makes neater stripes without any jagged edges. This striped scarf with pompom trim is worked horizontally, which means you need to cast on loads of stitches (200 for the scarf) but only knit for 10in (25cm) before casting off. It's just one of three options: the others are a plain scarf and a cowl. Her instructions are clear and annotated, but if you'd like to print off a pdf pattern, one is provided.

H. 1/16

The Author

Tessa Evelegh is a magazine and newspaper journalist in the UK. She is the author of over 30 books which include *Sewing Made Simple* and the bestselling *The Great British Sewing Bee*, launched with the BBC2 series.

Picture Credits

The publishers would like to thank the following sources for their kind permission to reproduce the pictures in this book.

All images are from Shutterstock except for the following:

Page 9 Donna Wolfe from Naztazia; 10 Kietisak/Thinkstock; 11 Serezniy/Thinkstock; 13 VeryPinkKnits; 16 www.knitpicks.com; 19 Stylecraft; 21 © Carlton Books; 22 Jennlikesyarn; 25 Purl Soho, 459 Broome St, New York, NY 10013. Websites: purlsoho.com & purlbee.com; 27 VeryPinkKnits; 29 VeryPinkKnits; 34 Liat Gat; 35 Video content created and owned by Genevieve Hudak, Astraknots LLC, www.astraknots.com; 36 Knitca; 37 © Carlton Books; 38 VeryPinkKnits; 39 VeryPinkKnits; 40 Wikimedia Commons; 41 © Carlton Books; 43 Video content created and owned by Genevieve Hudak, Astraknots LLC, www.astraknots.com; 46 VeryPinkKnits; 47 VeryPinkKnits; 50 EasterBunnyUK/Thinkstock; 58 VeryPinkKnits; 60 VeryPinkKnits; 61 PlanetPurl; 63 © Carlton Books; 64 © Carlton Books; 66 Barol16/Thinkstock; 67 Pleasntseas; 70 Lisa Savage knitsandnotions.com; 71 Rex Features; 73 Judy Graham; 74 PlanetPurl; 75 PlanetPurl; 76 PlanetPurl; 77 iknitwithcatfur; 78 PlanetPurl; 80 Knitca; 81 VeryPinkKnits; 82 Deepak Aggarwal/Getty Images; 83 Peter Crowther/Getty Images; 85 Rebecca Roush Brown from ChemKnits; 86 VeryPinkKnits; 88 © Carlton Books; 89 Alexis Winslow; 90 Kyoko Nakayoshi, Cotton & Cloud, www.cottonandcloud.com; 91 www.knitpicks.com; 97 Michelle 'Knit Purl' Hunter; 98 Cheryl Brunette; 100 KnittingHelp.com; 102 Jimmy Beans Wool; 103 Cheryl Brunette; 105 VeryPinkKnits; 110 iknitwithcatfur; 111 Chia Chong – chiachong.com; 112 Christy Hills; 113 Kristen McDonnell of Studio Knit; 115 www.knitpicks.com; 116 www.knitpicks.com; 117 Wool and the Gang; 118 Simplymaggie.com; 120 Sheep & Stitch; 121 Christy Hills; 124 Pleasntseas; 125 Pleasntseas; 126 VeryPinkKnits; 127 The Casting on the Couch, www.castingonthecouch.com.

Every effort has been made to acknowledge correctly and contact the source and/or copyright holder of each picture and Carlton Books Limited apologizes for any unintentional errors or omissions, which will be, corrected in future editions of this book.